Harriet Westbrook Shelley

Harriet Shelley's Letters to Catherine Nugent

Harriet Westbrook Shelley

Harriet Shelley's Letters to Catherine Nugent

ISBN/EAN: 9783337106805

Printed in Europe, USA, Canada, Australia, Japan

Cover: Foto ©ninafisch / pixelio.de

More available books at **www.hansebooks.com**

HARRIET SHELLEY'S

LETTERS

TO

CATHERINE NUGENT.

London:

Printed for Private Circulation.

1889.

CONTENTS.

CONTENTS.

PREFACE.

The following letters were communicated by Mr. Alfred Webb of Dublin to the New York paper entitled *The Nation*, in which they appeared, in two instalments, on the 6th and 13th of June 1889. Mr. Webb mentions that Catherine Nugent, to whom the letters were addressed, was forty years old in 1812, when she was shop-assistant to "one Newman, a furrier, who carried on business at No. 101 Grafton Street," Dublin. During the Irish campaign of Shelley, Harriet became intimate with Catherine Nugent; and the intimacy led to the correspondence of which one side forms the present volume.

Mr. Webb says he copied the letters eight years ago from the originals in the possession of Catherine Nugent's niece, and that the death of the said Catherine's "only representative now renders possible their publication." * They are certainly worth preserving in the form of a book, though it may not be desirable at present to do more than print a few copies for private circulation.

The book forms in fact an important body of evidence as to the kind of person that Shelley's first wife was, and the character of the relations which existed between the young couple. The letters were spread over almost three years; and they show an unbroken friendship on the part of the young wife towards the middle-aged furrier's assistant, and a friendship gradually deepening into affection. The earlier letters convey the impression that Harriet fancied herself a republican simply because she had married one, and that her enthusiasm for Catherine Nugent arose from Shelley's; but this impression gradually dies out as we find Harriet recounting to the little Irish

---

* *The Nation*, vol. xlviii, pp. 164—165.

seamstress and philanthropist one after another
of the awakenings undergone by the young married couple in regard to the various people with
whom they came in contact. And at last Harriet's
own sad awakening from her two years' dream of
domestic happiness is revealed to the same friend,
to whom she still clings affectionately. That she
was capable of warmth and constancy is evident ;
that she passed two years of happiness with Shelley,
she told Catherine Nugent in unmistakeable terms
before the cloud had arisen ; and, when the storm
burst that laid waste that happiness, she gave the
same friend her version of the affair in equally
unmistakeable terms. She thought Shelley wholly
changed in character, and blamed Mary Godwin
for artfully contriving the disunion.

The whole series of letters, happy and unhappy, presents a pleasing portrait of Harriet,
artlessly drawn by her own hand, and giving
an impression of frankness and genuineness.
The impression may perhaps be erroneous, or
Harriet may have been mistaken in her views
about Shelley and Mary ; but it will be very
difficult to convince those who regard Shelley as
the aggressor that the young wife who wrote

b

these letters had any reason to deem herself
wanting in her duty and affection towards
him.

LONDON:

August 1st, 1889.

LETTERS.

B

LETTERS

TO

CATHERINE NUGENT.

---◆---

LETTER I.

17 Grafton St.,
[Dublin].
Wedndy.

To MRS. NUGENT.

If you are not engaged will you give us your company this eveng., as Mr. S. is not at home. Bring your work.

Yours truly,
H. S.

LETTER II.

17 Grafton Street.

[Dublin].

Sundy. Morning.

Mrs. Shelley's compts. to Mrs. Nugent, and expects the pleasure of her company to dinner, 5 O'clock, as a murdered chicken has been prepared for her repast.

LETTER III.

Direct NANTGUILTE,
    RHAYADER, RADNORSHIRE, South Wales.
                April 16th [1812].

My Dear Mrs. Nugent,

After travelling over an immense tract of country in the hopes of finding a house in which it would be our greatest joy to welcome a *native of that country* so dear to my recollection, though at the same time so painful to the feelings of one who unfortunately, being an *Englishwoman,* must never hope to see realized her warmest wishes in behalf of a *nation* so deserving of every happiness which this and the next world can afford. You know when we left Dublin the wind was against us : but by making several tacks we contrived to get out of harbour, and continued sailing 36 hours when we had been informed that at the most we should certainly be no more than 12 hours. There is no dependence upon the word of a sailor, you may have heard me say, and now I am more confirmed in it. We did not arrive at Holyhead till near 2 O'clock on Monday morning. Then we had above a mile to walk over rocks and stone in a pouring mist before we could get to the inn. The night was dark and stormy: but the sailors had lanterns, or else I think it would have been better to have remained on board. As soon as we could get supper we did. We did not eat anything for 36 hours all the time we were on board, and immediately began *upon meat;* you will think this very extraordinary, but Percy and my sister suffered so much by the voyage, and were so much weakened by the vegetable system, that had they still continued it would have been seeking a premature grave. I fared the best of any as I slept most part of the time. On Tuesday we began travelling and that day week we found our way here. Strange as it may appear, we have been all through North Wales to find a house, but not one presented itself, nor should we have this if a very unpleasant circumstance had not taken place. The person to whom it belongs was a sea captain, and a brother in law of his has involved him in bankruptcy by very unfair means, and has himself absconded with £2,000, therefore now all this man's property is to go to satisfy the creditors. He was his partner in this country's bank and has defrauded many people of their money. The beauty of this place is not to be described. It is quite an old family house, with a farm of 200 acres meadow land. The rent is £98 a year, which we think very cheap ; but by letting a part of the farm we can reduce it to £20 per annum. I must now say adieu. We all unite in kind regards, and believe me your sincere *friend*

H. S.

LETTER IV.

Direct CUM ELAN,

RHAYADER, RADNORSHIRE, S.W.

June 7th [1812.]

My dear Mrs. Nugent,

So long a time has passed since we have had the pleasure of hearing from you that the various conjectures arising in our minds as to the cause require explanation. I am sure of this, should you chance to receive my letter. But in the meantime let me tell you all our disappointments. First, then you will see from the date of this that we are not at our beloved Nantgwylt. Alas that charming spot is, I am afraid, never destined to be ours! The possessor cannot settle with Percy, and indeed he has acted such a *villanous* part that we have been obliged to leave him, and for a few days take up our residence at Mr. Groves, about a mile and a half from our favourite residence. You may imagine our sorrow at leaving so desirable a spot, where every beauty seems centred. I had hoped to have seen you there; but I am afraid I must relinquish and with sorrow so fallacious a wish. We have some thoughts of going to Italy till Percy is of age, as the same difficulty will attend us wherever we. [*sic*] One very great inducement to go to Italy is the warmth of the climate, as Percy's health is so extremely delicate that the cold air of this country is not likely to benefit him. What have you thought upon the murder of the Prime Minister? Undoubtedly it was very distressing, but the man's composure is astounding. I think he was a Methodist from his behaviour. I am sorry for his family. It had been better if they had killed Lord Castlereagh. He really deserved it; but this poor Mr. P. I believe was a very good private character. Do you not think it nonsense for all the little towns and villages to send petitions to the Prince upon the occasion. I suppose Ireland has not done anything half so silly. How do your poor countrymen go on? I hope things are not so scarce there as here. How very lovely the weather is now. Summer comes at last and with it brings its disappointment,

for you are not the only one I had hoped to have
seen at Nantgwylt. Godwin's children were to
come to us ; but our evil genius has stepped in
and forbid us that happiness. We are to begin
travelling again soon and where to bend our steps
I know not ; but we think of going to the seaside
until our passports come. We must remain here
until we receive remittances from London. Percy
is related to Mr. Grove, and his wife is a very
pleasant woman, tho' too formal to be agreeable.
He is a very proud man. Therefore you may
guess how we pass our time. Do you ever see
Mr. Lawless ? We hear from him sometimes. As
to the poems I have no idea how and when they
will come out. The printers are very slow in their
operations. I must now conclude in hopes of
hearing from you soon. Believe me your sincere,
affectionate friend

H. S.

Percy and Eliza desire to be remembered.

LETTER V.

Direct LYMOUTH,
near BARNSTAPLE, Devonshire.
June 30th [1812.]

My dear Mrs. Nugent,

Now that we are again settled I take up the pen in the hope of giving that pleasure which I receive from reading your letter. I received it during my stay at Cum Elan and a few days after we left that lovely spot, and its amiable hostess for a journey to Chepstow, where we were in hopes of finding a house that would suit us, and where we might with pleasure receive the visit of one whose presence like the sun would make happy those who beheld her. Your letter damped the joy I felt from reading it, by seeing that you could not come to us this summer, for I had hoped tho' we had left Nangwylt that we should have been sure of a visit from you. However, I will say no more about it, as you must be the best judge of your own affairs, and I doubt not that were we to draw you from your own country we should be the means, tho' innocently, of depriving many of your unfortunate countrymen of that relief you know so well how to bestow. I will say this though I am a loser by it. Continue, oh amiable woman, the path marked out to thee by virtue and humanity, and let not the whisperings of selfishness in us take thee from so laudable an undertaking. We may yet meet ere this world shall close our eyes, and that we both desire it our hearts are the best judges. I will now tell you how we came into Devonshire. We arrived at Chepstow. We found the house not half built, and by no means large enough for our family. I did not regret it, as the country was by no means beautiful. We then proceeded into this country, and came to this place on our way to Ilfracombe, and the beauty of it has made us residents here for the summer months, when we think of going to London for the winter. It combines all the beauties of our late residence with the addition of a fine, bold sea. We have taken the only cottage there was, which is most beautifully situated, commanding a fine view of the sea, with mountains at the side and behind us. Vegetation is more luxuriant here than in any part of England. We have roses and myrtles creeping up the sides of the house, which is thatched at the top. It is such a little place that it seems more like a fairy scene than anything in reality. All the houses are built in the cottage style, and I suppose there are not more than thirty in all. We send to Barnstaple for everything, and our letters come but twice a week. It is eighteen miles from Barnstaple, therefore one ought to be able to [*paper torn*] very well on a horse to get there. We have an immense precipice to descend into this valley, about two miles in length, which no carriage can come down. It seems as if nature had intended that this place should be so romantic and shut out from all other intercourse with the neighbouring villages and towns. We have still our Irishman Daniel, whom you may remember in Grafton Street. I am afraid we shall be obliged to part with him, as we do not find him that useful servant we expected he would have [*sic*] Percy has some thoughts of sending him to Dublin, to see after his poems that are at the printers; but whether he will or not is impossible to say. We have not heard from Mr. Lawless now for some time. I suppose his present employment to my idea not very laudable, fills up his time so much that he cannot think of his absent friends. I hope this is not the case as I should be sorry, knowing him to be an Irishman, if it were true. I think he is a man of very great talent and abilities; but I am afraid that Mr. Curran will never lend him a helping hand. I must now say adieu, my dear friend, and may you ever feel that happiness which springs from conscious integrity and goodness of heart. Percy and Eliza desire to be most kindly remembered, and believe me ever your truly sincere and affectionate friend

HARRIET.

LETTER VI.

LYNMOUTH.
August 4th [1812].

My dear Mrs. Nugent,

Your affectionate letter gave us very great pleasure. To hear from those we love when it is not in our power to see them constitutes one of the greatest joys in existence. You may suppose how we laughed at the idea of the tempter, tho' how such a horrible looking creature should gain admittance to the garden of Eden at once surprises me and turns the sanctity of the whole into a burlesque. I suppose the ingenious discoverer has very good reasons and arguments to support his cause, tho' we may doubt if we like, the idea is truly ridiculous and laughable and how do the people take this new mode of accounting for how all the sin in the world arose. Will they believe

it as soon as they would the other? If they do
I should be inclined to think their belief is a mere
matter of form and not an involuntary act. If
they go on in this way we shall next hear, I suppose, of its being a bear or lion or anything else.
I thank you in Percy's name for your kind offer
of service, though at the same time we cannot
accept it. The case is this. His printer refuses
to go on with his poems until he is paid. Now
such a demand is seldom made, as printers are
never paid till the profits arising from the work
come in, and Percy agreed with him to this effect,
and as long as we staid in Dublin he wore the
mask which is now taken off. However I am in
great hopes that Mr. Lawless will get them from
him. He is coming to London on business and
then we shall see him. I wish to think well of
him because he is your countryman, tho' there is
too much "the man of the world" about him.
Perhaps he is different out of the city. If not,
I shall still admire his talents, tho' I shall have
no high opinion of him. What do you think of
Cobbett? A man that can change his opinions so
quickly I do not admire, and particularly when he
could write of Sir F. Burdett in such an abusive

and contradictory a way. It seems to me that Cobbett merely changes his sentiments as occasion requires as best suits his interest. I hope I am mistaken, tho' his behaviour looks very like it. Percy has sent you a defense of D. F. Eaton. It must not be published, but you will give us your opinion of it. What think you of Lord Stanhope? —divine being, how beautifully he speaks. We have sent him one as well as Sir F. Burdett. Did you see a clergyman enter into his defence? I do not remember his name, but it was a very wonderful thing to hear a clergyman write for universal toleration. He said his standing in the pillory was an honour to him. I think the publick mind is very much in favour of Mr. Eaton. It looks well, does it not? Our friend Miss Hitchener is come to us. She is very busy writing for the good of mankind. She is very dark in complexion with a great quantity of long black hair. She talks a great deal. If you like great talkers she will suit you. She is taller than me or my sister, and as thin as it is possible to be. I hope you will see her some day. I should think that next summer you might take a peep at us. You may judge how much we all wish to

D

see you. Your being an Irishwoman must interest us in your happiness independently of our
knowing the amiable qualities you possess. I
have read Miss Owenson's "Missionary" and
much do I admire the author. I am now reading
her "Novice of St. Dominick." I regret not
having known her when I was in Dublin. Her
patriotic sketches have won my heart. She speaks
so feelingly of your dear country that I love her
for that. Miss Hitchiner has read your letter
and loves you in good earnest. Her own ex-
pression. I know you would love her did you
know her. Her age is thirty. She looks like as
if she was only twenty-four and her spirits are
excellent. She laughs, and talks and writes all
day. She has seen the Godwins and thinks
Godwin different to what he seems, he lives so
much from his family, only seeing them at stated
hours. We do not like that; and he thinks
himself such a very great man. He would not
let one of his children come to us, just because he
had not seen our faces. Just as if writing to a
person in which we express all our thoughts, was
not a sufficient knowledge of them. I know our
friend whom we call *Bessy* just as well when we

corresponded as I do now. Such excuses sit not well upon so great a literary character as he is. I might have expected such an excuse from a woman of selfish and narrow mind, but not from Godwin. I must now finish. They all unite in love and affection to our dear little Irishwoman, and believe me more than ever your sincerely attached and affectionate friend

H. S.

LETTER VII.

LYMOUTH.
August 11th [1812].

My dear Mrs. Nugent,

Your friend and our friend *Bessey* has been reading pieces of Irish history and is so much enraged with the characters there mentioned that nothing will satisfy her desire of revenge but the printing and publishing of them to exhibit to the world those characters which are (shameful to say) held up as beings possessing every amiable quality, whilst their hearts are as bad as it is possible to be. They will be shown to the world in a new light, and it will remain to be seen if that world does not repay them as they so eminently deserve. Percy thinks of printing it by subscription. 500 subscribers at seven shillings each will amply repay the printing and publishing.

Percy intends to print some proposals for printing Pieces of Irish History, saying that every one whether Irish or English ought to read them. We depend upon you for many subscribers, as being upon the spot where so many of your exalted and brave countrymen suffered martyrdom. I should think there were very many would be glad to put their names to it. There must be many still smarting under the wounds they have seen their brave companions suffer, and all from this hated country of mine. Good God, were I an Irishman or woman how I should hate the English. It is wonderful how the poor Irish people can tolerate them. But I am writing to one who from her example shows them how they ought to tolerate this barbarous nation of ours. Thank God we are not all alike, for I too can hate Lord Castlereagh as much as any Irishwoman. How does my heart's blood run cold at the idea of what he did in your unfortunate country. How is it that man is suffered to walk the streets in open daylight I Oh if I were to meet him I really think I could fly at him, and tear him to pieces I I have drawn a likeness of him and Percy says it is a very good one. You know I have no pretensions to drawing; but sometimes I take up the pen and sketch faces. I have not preserved the horrible countenance but if I were to meet it I should it for him [*sic*]. I cannot bear Curran; what use is he to your country? Was he active at the time of the Union? No! if he had been, though his life had been the sacrifice, Ireland would have been saved. I have no patience with Curran. I shall convert Mr. *Lawless* I hope from his *idol*. It is too sickening to hear him talk of Curran as he does. We are going to the valley of Llangothlin. It is much nearer to Ireland than we are here or even at Nangwylt. If we are there next summer I hope we shall see you. Bessy wishes very much to see you. Your last letter won her heart instantly. Reading "Pieces of Irish History" has made her so low-spirited. She possesses too much feeling for her own happiness. I am in great hopes she will get the better of her low spirits. May I ask how are your spirits and your health? If they are but as good as I wish them to be it will make me very happy. You do not let your feelings get the better of your reason. If you do I am extremely sorry, as I shall know from that you are not so happy as you ought to be. They all unite in the kindest regards to the dear little Irish-woman, and believe me most sincerely your attached friend

H. S.

[*Note added by P. B. Shelley.*]

I shall print proposals for publishing by sub-scription, and if you could send us any names you would much benefit the *cause.* We determine at any rate to publish the Irish History. It is a matter of doubt with me whether any bookseller will dare to put his name to it. This will be no obstacle.

LETTER VIII.

LEWIS'S HOTEL,

    ST. JAMES'S STREET, LONDON. [1812].

My dear Mrs. Nugent,

You will smile at my address, wondering how and where we have been during the long interval which has taken place since the receipt of your last letter. I believe I mentioned that we were going to the Vale of Langothlin there to remain at least for the winter season; but I know not how it is that whenever we fix upon any particular place of residence something comes to take us to another. Instead of going to Langothlin we went to a New town which is called Tremadoc. It is built upon and that has been saved from the sea by a Mr. Madock*, M.P. for Boston. The character of this man is such as to call forth our warmest admiration

---

* Mr. W. Alexander Madocks.

and esteem. He is what we call a true *patriot* in every sense of the word. He loves his country dearly and always stands up for the interests and welfare of the poor. He is building an embankment which does honour to him and is an ornament to his country ; but unfortunately possessing only a small fortune, when compared with the immense sums that others possess, he has not sufficient to finish the undertaking which has cost him twelve years hard labour. We came up to London in the hopes of raising a subscription that would finish ; but as yet nothing is done. Bysshe's being a minor lays us under many unpleasant affairs and makes us obliged to depend upon in a great measure the will of others, in the manner of raising money, and without which nothing is to be done. We have seen the Godwins. Need I tell you that I love them all ? You have read his works therefore you know how you feel towards the author. His manners are so soft and pleasing that I defy even an enemy to be displeased with him. We have the pleasure of seeing him daily, and upon his account we determined to settle near London. For long journeys do not agree with him, having never been in the habit of travelling when a young man.

E

There is one of the daughters of that dear Mary Wolstoncroft living with him. She is 19 years of age, very plain, but very sensible. The beauty of her mind fully overbalances the plainness of her countenance. There is another daughter of hers, who is now in Scotland. She is very much like her mother, whose picture hangs up in his study. She must have been a most lovely woman. Her countenance speaks her a woman who would dare to think and act for herself. I wish you could share the pleasure we enjoy in his company. He is quite a family man. He has one son by his present wife, a little boy of nine years old. He is extremely clever, and will, I have no doubt, follow the same enlightened path that Godwin has before him. Godwin is particularly fond of Curran, and I am to be introduced to Miss Curran on Sunday. How comes [or came, paper torn *] in England, can you solve this problem? You know that Mrs. Godwin keeps a bookseller's shop. She conducts the whole herself. I am in great hopes she will succeed. They are sometimes very much

---

* *Query.* The line should perhaps be: "How came she (Miss Curran) to be in England, can you solve this problem?"

pressed for enough ready money. They require such an immense capital; but taking every thing as it goes, I think they will succeed. The many trials that Mrs. Godwin has had to encounter make me very much inclined to believe her a woman of great fortitude and unyielding temper of mind. There is a very great sweetness marked in her countenance. In many instances she has shown herself a woman of very great magnanimity and independence of character. Oh if you could see them all to-morrow. I am going to stay all day with them. G. is very much taken with Percy. He seems to delight so much in his society. He has given up everything for the sake of our society. It gives me so much pleasure to sit and look at him. Have you ever seen a bust of Socrates, for his head is very much like that? Percy, Bessey and Eliza desire to be remembered most affectionately to you. Percy says he wishes you to go to Stockdales, and get all his manuscript poems and other pieces. I am afraid you will be obliged to use a little man-œuvre to get them. In the first place you can say you wish to look at them, and then you may be able to stout them away from him. I leave it all to you, knowing you will do your best, in the way

to obtain them, and believe me ever most sincerely
your attached friend

H. SHELLEY.

P.S. If I have said anything wrong pray forgive
me.

LETTER IX.

STRATFORD UPON AVON.

November 14th [1812].

My dear Mrs. Nugent,

My last letter to you was from London, which place I left on Friday the 13th, and am now on my way to Tanyralt our beautiful Welsh cottage. The reasons of your silence I am at a loss to account for. Unless your answer has not been delivered to me, a circumstance not at all impossible, considering the hotel we lodged at. Do not think from this that we are backward in our enquiries every day respecting letters. They are and always will be the first objects of our solicitude, when coming from so dear a friend as yourself. The lady I have so often mentioned to you, of the name of Hitchener, has to our very great happiness left us. We were entirely deceived

in her character as to republicanism, and in short
everything else which she pretended to be. We
were not long in finding out our great disappointment in her. As to any noble disinterested views
it is utterly impossible for a selfish character to
feel them. She built all her hopes on being able
to separate me from my dearly loved Percy, and
had the artfulness to say that Percy was really in
love with her, and it was only his being married
that could keep her within bounds now. Percy had
seen her once before his marriage. He thought
her sensible but nothing more. She wrote con-
tinually, and at last I wrote to her, and was very
much charmed with her letters. We thought it a
thousand pities such a mind as hers appeared
to be should be left in a place like that she in-
habited. We therefore were very urgent for her
to come and live with us; which was no sooner
done than we found out our mistake. It was a
long time ere we could possibly get her away, till
at last Percy said he would give her £100 per
annum. And now thank God she has left us
never more to return. We are much happier now
than all the time she was with us. Have you been
able to get the poems from Stockdale? If not it

cannot be helped, but do pray write to us, for we are quite uneasy at not hearing from you for so long a time. Direct your letters to me at Tanyralt, near the town of Tremadoc (in Carnarvonshire, North Wales). It is 260 miles from London, but the loveliest place I have seen many a day. We are not very far from Ireland. If you could so manage it as to come to us in the Spring, you know not the happiness you would confer upon our little circle, which is now just as you beheld it in your own native air. I have got the Irish Melodies, which I intend to study. If you know of any good old Irish song I should esteem it a favor to hear of it. I must now say adieu, and believe me truly your affectionate friend

H. S.

Percy and Eliza desire not to be forgotten.

LETTER X.

TAN-Y-RALLT.

Jany. 16th [1813].

My dear Mrs. Nugent,

The sight of your well known hand was like intelligence from the dead to the living. Shall I say that it gave me only pleasure? no, that is too cold a word to convey the feelings of happiness, in which we all alike participated. I am sorry to hear you have been so much engaged, as I cannot bear the idea of a woman like yourself being obliged to do that which so many are better qualified to perform. I saw with very great sorrow the ruin of so many of your valuable manufactories. I knew how many of your unfortunate countrymen suffered all the miseries of famine before, and now there must be many more. That the wounds of thy beloved country may soon be healed for ever,

is the first wish of an Englishwoman who only
regrets her being born among those inhuman
beings who have already caused so much misery
wherever they turn their steps. All the good I
wrote of Mr. Madocks I recant. I find I have been
dreadfully deceived respecting that man. We are
now living in his house, where formerly nothing
but folly and extravagance reigned. Here they
held their midnight revels, insulting the spirit of
nature's sublime scenery. The sea which used to
dash against the most beautiful grand rocks, for
grand indeed they are, and the mind is lost in
contemplation of them towering above one another,
and on the opposite side the most jagged mountains, whose peaks are generally covered in clouds,
was to please his stupid vanity and to celebrate his
name, turned from its course, and now we have for
a fine bold sea which there used to be, nothing but
a sandy marsh uncultivated and ugly to the view.
How poor does this work of man seem when
standing on one of the mountains we see them all
rising one behind the other looking as tho' they
had stood the iron grasp of time many centuries.
Then to look down on this embankment which
viewed from the height looks as if a puff of wind

from the mountains would send it to oblivion like its founder's name. The harm that man has done through his extravagance is incalculable. Here he built the town of Tremadoc, and then almost ruined its shopkeepers by never paying their just debts. We have been the means of saving the bank from utter destruction, for which I am extremely glad, as that person who purchases it will reap very great benefit from it. I admire your song much, and am determined to set it to some very plaintive* tune. I have seen Miss Curran: she resides in England. What I saw of her I did not like. She said begging was a trade in Dublin. To tell you the truth she is not half such an Irishwoman as myself, and that is why I did not feel disposed to like her. Besides she is a coquette the most abominable thing in the world. I met her at Godwin's house alas [paper torn] Godwin he too is changed, and filled with prejudices, and besides too he expects such universal homage from all persons younger than himself, that it is very disagreeable to be in company with him on that account, and he wanted Mr. Shelley to join

---

* "*Plaintiff*" in the *Nation* version.

the Tory party and do just as they pleased, which made me very angry, as we know what men the Tories are, now. He is grown old and unimpassioned, therefore is not in the least calculated for such enthusiasts as we are. He has suffered a great deal for his principles, but that ought to make him more staunch in them, at least it would me. Eliza and Percy desire their kind regards to you, with many thanks for your embassy to Stockdale, who will hear from Mr. S. soon. Adieu, dearest friend to liberty and truth, and that you may ever be happy is the first prayer of your affectionate friend

H. SHELLEY.

COOKE's HOTEL.

ALBEMARLE-STREET, LONDON.

May 21st [1813].

My dear Mrs. Nugent,

I find the longer a time elapses before I make my apology for not having written before, the more awkward I feel at the idea of addressing you. My greatest consolation, however, is derived from this—that you will not attribute my silence to neglect, but to the hurry and bustle of a city. I am ashamed to say I have written to no one since I arrived here, if that can extenuate my crime. You would pardon me if you knew in what a scene of confusion I live. To give a description of it is impossible. Even now there are two waiters in the room to lay our cloth for dinner, and you well know the movements of a waiter are far from silent. I have been in London a long time, though it seems to me that I have only been here a few days. Mr. Shelley's family are very eager to be reconciled to him, and I should not in the least wonder if my next letter was not sent from his paternal roof, as we expect to be there in a week or two. His father has been in town, when, at the earnest solicitation of his cousin, Bysshe wrote to him. He has not yet answered the letter; but we expect it daily. Their conduct is most surprising, after treating us like dogs they wish for our Society. I hope it will turn out well, tho' I hardly dare suppose so. My sister has joined me some time. You may suppose I was not a little pleased to see her again. We have not got our boxes yet, that were sent from Cork to Bristol, and when we shall see them again is uncertain. Mr. Ryan dines with us to-day. I give him meat, but we have all taken to the vegetable regimen again, which I shall not leave off, for I find myself so much better for it, that it would be very great injustice to eat flesh again. Have you seen Mr. Lawless? He wrote to us from prison a few weeks ago, but I do not suppose he was there,

because Ryan knew nothing about it, and he is
only just arrived from there. This is franked by
La Touche, for I feel it is not worth postage. I
hope to hear from you soon, tho' I feel I do not
deserve it; but you are too kind to take any
advantage over me. Mr. Shelley continues perfectly
well, and his poem of Queen Mab is begun, tho' it
must not be published under pain of death, because
it is too much against every existing establishment.
It is to be privately distributed to his friends, and
some copies sent over to America. Do you
[qy. know] any one that would wish for so dan-
gerous a gift? If you do, tell me of them, and
they shall not be forgotten. Adieu! All unite
in kind regards to you, and I remain your sincerely
attached friend

                                   H. SHELLEY.

Direct to this hotel.

LETTER XII.

COOKES HOTEL.
DOVER STREET, PICCADILLY.
June 22nd [1813].

My dear Mrs. Nugent,

The kind expressions contained in your last letter gave me sincere pleasure, feeling as I did that I had not acted according to my ideas of right and wrong in delaying writing to you. I am sorry to hear that poor Lawless is confined. If he had taken his friends' advice all his debts would have been settled long ago; but pride, that bane of all human happiness, unfortunately stopped and marred all his good prospects. Mr. Ryan is still in London; but I expect to hear daily of his leaving us. Have you had any good weather, for ours is miserable? our summer has not yet commenced. The fruit is still sour for want of sun,

and will continue so from the present appearance
of the weather.   Our Irish servant is going to
leave.   Poor fellow, he pines after his dear Ireland, and is at the same time very ill.   He was
never of any use to us; but so great was his at-
tachment that we could not bear to send him
away.   Mr. Shelley has broken off the negocia-
tion, and will have no more to say to his son,
because that son will not write to the people of
Oxford, and declare his return to Christianity.
Did you ever hear of such an old dotard?   It
seems that so long as he lives, Bysshe must never
hope to see or hear anything of his family.   This
is certainly an unpleasant circumstance, particularly as his mother wishes to see him, and has
a great affection for him.   What think you of
Bonaparte?   To most of the Irish he is a great
favourite : I only wish we had peace.   So long a
war as this has been is indeed too dreadful to
continue much longer.   How is your health?   I
am afraid you sit too close to your business to
enjoy good health ; yet, as the winter is gone,
surely you need not make any more warm tippets !
That will be time enough next November.   We
have not seen much of Godwin, for his wife is so

dreadfully disagreeable that I could not bear the idea of seeing her. Mr. S. has done that away, tho', by telling G. that I could not bear the society of his darling wife. Poor man, we are not the only people who find her troublesome. Mr. S. joins me and Eliza in kind regards to you, and believe me yours with esteem

H. S.

G

Letter XIII.

High Elms House,
    Bracknell, Berkshire.
                August 8th [1813].

My dear Mrs. Nugent,

I confess I have been guilty of seeming unkindness in not writing before; but such a multiplicity of business has occupied me ever since the receipt of your last that I have not had a moment to spare, even to you, my kind friend. The babe * is quite well, and very much grown. She is indebted to you for many kind enquiries, which one day she will thank you for in person. Mr. S. is of age; but no longer heir to the immense property of his sires. They are trying to take it away, and will I am afraid succeed, as it appears there is a flaw in the drawing up of the settlement, by which they

---

* Ianthe Elizabeth.

can deprive him of everything. This is a beautiful idea, and well worthy the noble men who have formed it, among whom I suspect a certain *great personage*. They have put it into Chancery, tho' I fancy it can and will be kept an entire secret. You may suppose that he will do everything to prevent this shameful abuse of property, as we are convinced that more good would be effected if we have it, than if they regain it. We are now in a house 30 miles from London, merely for convenience. How long we remain is uncertain, as I fear our necessities will oblige us to remove to a greater distance. Our friends the Newtons are trying to do everything in their power to serve us; but our doom is decided. You who know us well may judge of our feelings. To have all our plans set aside in this manner is a miserable thing. Not that I regret the loss, but for the sake of those I intended to benefit. Mr. S. unites with me and Eliza in kind regards, whilst believe me your firmly attached friend

H. S.

HIGH ELMS HOUSE,
BRACKNELL, BERKS.
Sept. 10 [1813].

My dear Mrs. Nugent,

I hasten to answer your last letter and to give you the same hopes which we entertain about the subject of my last. Mr. Shelley has seen his Father and told him of what he heard, which he denied, and received him very kindly. Since then his lawyer has employed a council (*sic*). His opinion is at present pending. I have no doubt now, tho' I had at first, that they can take it away. I have a very bad opinion of all lawyers in general, and I rather think Mr. S's lawyer was either told so by some one, or he thought it necessary to employ a council. They are for ever playing a losing game into each others hands. I am very sorry to hear you have been so ill. I hope sincerely you will soon recover, and do not, I pray you, sit so close to your business; for it is not one that contributes to the happiness of the many, only ·the few, who ought not, in my opinion, to indulge in such useless luxuries at the expense of so many who are even now at a loss for food. Of late we have had many arguments concerning the respect that all men pay to property. Now what do you think of this affair? I wish much to know if your ideas on this subject correspond with ours! I will not tell you what they are yet as I have an excellent reason which you will acknowledge when you hear it. The post has just brought me a letter from Mr. Shelley's sister, who says that her father is doing all in his power to prevent his being arrested. I think even his family pride must long to give way on the present occasion. [*Paper torn*] keeps everything a secret, but Mrs. Shelley tells her son everything she hears. I will write again soon and tell you everything that takes place. With every good wish for your happiness, in which we all unite, believe me most affectionately your friend

H. SHELLEY.

We think of going to our favourite Nantgwilt, but not yet. You will certainly hear from me again at this house before we can go. Let me hear from you soon.

LETTER XV.

SUNDAY,
October 11th [1813].

My dear Mrs. Nugent,

We are again among our dear mountains. One week has sufficed to perform a journey of more than 300 miles, with my sweet babe, who I am most happy to say has received no injury from the journey. I am now staying at Lowwood Inn, which is close to the Lake of Windermere in Westmoreland. We do not wish any one to know where we are. Therefore if any one should ask you I rely upon [your] friendship for not satisfying their curiosity. Have you seen Daniel? We were obliged to discharge him, for his conduct was so unprincipled that it was impossible to have him in our service any longer. Is Mr. Lawless out of prison yet? Had he not taken us in as he did, Bysshe

would have done something for him; but his
behaviour was altogether so dishonest that Mr.
Shelley will not do anything for him at present.
If he wished it he could not, for he is obliged to
pay 3 for 1, which is so ruinous that he will only
raise a sufficient [sum] to pay his debts. In November
he is to see his father; but I do not expect they
will settle anything, for Mr. S. will never give way
to his son in the least. How has your health been
since I heard from you last! I sincerely hope you
are better, and that you will take care of yourself,
I wish you could see my sweet babe. She is so fair,
with such sweet blue eyes, that the more I see her
the more beautiful she looks. Some day, my dear
friend, I hope you will come to England, and pay
us a visit. When we get our dear Nantgwilt, then
I may make sure of you. Mr. S. joins me and
Eliza in kind regards to you, and may you ever
be happy is the best and first wish of your sincere
friend

H. SHELLEY.

Direct your letter to me at Mrs. Calverts, Greta
Bank, Keswick, Cumberland.

LETTER XVI.

EDINBURGH,
October 20th [1813].

My dear Mrs. Nugent,

My last letter was written from the lakes of Cumberland, where we intended to stay still next ; but not finding any house that would suit us we came on to this far-famed city. A little more than two years has passed since I made my first visit here to be united to Mr. Shelley. To me they have been the happiest and the longest years of my life. The rapid succession of events since that time make the two years appear immeasurably long. I think the regular method of measuring time is by the number of different ideas which a rapid succession of events naturally give rise to. When I look back to the time before I was married I seem to feel I have lived a long time. Tho' my age is

H

but eighteen, yet I feel as if I was much older. Why are you so silent, my dear friend? I earnestly hope you are not ill. I am afraid it is nearly a month since I heard from you. I know well you would write oftener if you could. What is your employment on a Sunday? I think on those days you might snatch a few minutes to gratify my wishes. Do not direct your letter to me at Mrs. Calverts; but to the post office in this city. We think of remaining here all this winter. Tho' by no means fond of cities, yet I wished to come here, for when we went to the lakes we found such a set of human beings living there that it took off all our desire of remaining among the mountains. This City, is, I think, much the best. The people here are not so intolerant as they are in London. Literature stands on a higher footing here than anywhere else. My darling babe is quite well, and very much improved. Pray let me hear from you soon. Tell me if I can do anything for you. Mr. Shelley joins me and Eliza in kind regards to you, whilst I remain your affectionate friend

H. S.

Do not tell anyone where we are.

LETTER XVII.

No 36 FREDERICK-STREET,

EDINBURGH.

[*Postmark* "23 *Nov.* 1813."]

My dear Mrs. Nugent,

Your letter called forth the most lively feelings of regret. It is so long since I received a letter from you that I began to feel the greatest anxiety on your account. How much do I feel for your ill state of health. Tell me if I can be of any service to you. How are you situated with respect to personal comfort and attendance? Have you any-one by you who can sympathize with you? If you have not let me come and attend you. It is the office of a friend to soothe the languid moments of illness. The mind looks for sympathy more at such a time than when in perfect health. I am afraid Lawless has practised upon you, as he did

upon us. Some time back he wrote to Mr. S.
about Daniel, who lived with us, saying we had
not treated him well. Now the truth is this—we
were very fond of this man. He appeared so
much attached to us, with so much honesty and
simplicity, that we kept him tho' of no use what-
ever. For the whole time he stayed with us he
never did anything. Afterwards he turned out
very ungrateful, and behaved so insolently that we
were obliged to turn him away. This is the man
Lawless wrote about; but do not think I am
offended at what you say of him, as I know it
proceeds from the goodness of your heart. I only
wish the object was more deserving of your kind-
ness. There has been no conciliation between Mr.
[*paper torn* *] his father. Their opinions are so
contrary that I do not think there is the least
chance of their being reconciled. His father is
now ill with the gout; but there is no danger I
suppose. If there was he would send for his son
and be reconciled to him. I sincerely hope this
will find you better. You know what pleasure it
would give me to render you any service. There-

---

* *Probably* "Mr. Shelley and his father."

fore do not let a false opinion of justice keep you from applying to me in anything in which I can serve you. Mr. Shelley and Eliza join me in all good wishes for the recovery of your health; and believe me the most firmly, your attached friend

H. SHELLEY.

Letter XVIII.

(To Mrs. Newman.)

23 Chapel Street,

Grosvenor Square.

August 8th [1814].

Madam,

It is so long since I have heard from my amiable friend Mrs. Nugent, that I begin to fear she has quitted this world of sorrow and pain. If she has, no human being will regret her loss more than myself.. I must beg you to write by return of post and tell me all the particulars. If I am wrong in my conjectures tell her to write, if only one line to her most attached and faithful friend,

H. Shelley.

LETTER XIX.

23 CHAPEL STREET.

August 25th [1814].

My dear Mrs. Nugent,

I am afraid you will think I am not sincere, when I tell you what pleasure the sight of your handwriting caused me. I think as you do with the greatest horror on the present state of things —giving the slave trade to France for seven years. Can anything be more horrible? Peace has been hardly purchased at this price. I am dreadfully afraid America will never hold out against the numbers sent to invade her. How senseless all those rejoicings are! Deluded beings, they little know the many injuries that are to ensue. I expect France will soon have another revolution. The present King is not at all fitted to govern such a nation. Mr. Shelley is in France.* You will be surprised to find I am not with him; but times are altered, my dear friend, and tho' I will

* Shelley eloped with Mary Wollstonecraft Godwin the previous month.

not tell you what has passed, still do not think
that you cloud my mind with your sorrows. Every
age has its cares. God knows, I have mine. Dear
Ianthe is quite well. She is fourteen months old,
and has six teeth. What I should have done
without this dear babe and my sister I know not.
This world is a scene of heavy trials to us all. I
little expected ever to go through what I have.
But time heals the deepest wounds, and for the
sake of that sweet infant, I hope to live many
years. Write to me often. My dear friend you
know not what pleasure your letters give me. I
wish you lived in England that I might be near
you. Tell me how you are in health. Do not
despond. Tho' I see nothing to hope for when all
that was virtuous becomes vicious and depraved.
So it is—nothing is certain in this world. I suppose there is another where those that have suffered
heavily here will be happy. Tell me what you
think of this. My sister is with me. I wish you
knew her as well as I do. She is worthy of your
love. Now, dear friend, may you still be happy
is the first wish of your ever faithful friend,

H. SHELLEY.

Ianthe is well and very engaging.

LETTER XX.

23 CHAPEL STREET,
GROSVENOR SQUARE.
November 20th, [1814].

My dearest Mrs. Nugent,

Your fears are verified. Mr. Shelley has become profligate and sensual, owing entirely to Godwin's "Political Justice." The very great evil that book has done is not to be told. The false doctrines therein contained have poisoned many a young and virtuous mind. Mr. Shelley is living with Godwins two daughters—one by Mary Wolstoncraft, the other the daughter of his present wife, called Clairmont. I told you some time back Mr. S. was to give Godwin three thousand pounds. It was in effecting the accomplishment of this scheme that he was obliged to be at Godwins house, and Mary was determined

I

to secure him. She is to blame. She heated his imagination by talking of her mother, and going to her grave with him every day, till at last she told him she was dying in love for him, accompanied with the most violent gestures and vehement expostulations. He thought of me and my sufferings, and begged her to get the better of a passion as degrading to him as herself. She then told him she would die—he had rejected her, and what appeared to her as the sublimest virtue was to him a crime. Why could we not all live together? I as his sister, She as his wife? He had the folly to believe this possible, and sent for me, then residing at Bath. You may suppose how I felt at the disclosure. I was laid up for a fortnight after. I could do nothing for myself. He begged me to live. The doctors gave me over. They said 'twas impossible. I saw his despair. The agony of my beloved sister; and owing to the great strength of my constitution I lived; and here I am, my dear friend, waiting to bring another infant into this woful world. Next month I shall be confined. He will not be near me. No, he cares not for me now. He never asks after me or sends me word how he is going

on. In short, the man I once loved is dead. This
is a vampire. His character is blasted for ever.
Nothing can save him now. Oh! if you knew
what I have suffered, your heart would drop blood
for my miseries. When may I expect to see you?
Do tell me, my dear friend, and write soon. Eliza
is at Southampton with my darling babe. London
does not agree with her. Will you enquire for a
family of the name of Colthurst in Dublin? There
is one son and daughter growing up living with
the mother. I want the direction, as I know them
very well. Adieu, my dear friend, may you be
happy is the best wish of her who sincerely loves
you,

H. SHELLEY.

LETTER XXI.

23 CHAPEL STREET,

GROSVENOR SQUARE.

Decr. 11th, [1814].

My dearest Mrs. Nugent,

I have been confined a fortnight on Wednesday.
Ianthe has a brother. He is an eight month's
child, and very like his unfortunate father, who is
more depraved than ever. Oh my dear friend what
a dreadful trial it is to bring children into the world
so utterly helpless as he is, with no kind father's
care to heal the wounded frame. After so much
suffering my labour was a very good one, from
nine in the morning till nine at night. He is a
very healthy fine child for the time. I have seen
his father: he came to see me as soon as he knew
of the event ; but as to his tenderness for me, none
remains. He said he was glad it was a boy,

because he would make money cheaper. You see
how that noble soul is debased. Money now, and
not philosophy, is the grand spring of his actions.
Indeed the pure and enlightened philosophy he
once delighted in has flown. He is no longer that
pure and good being he once was, nor can he ever
retrieve himself. You will see us all in the Spring ;
I am about to come to Ireland, to get my boxes
which are detained there. You shall then return
with me to England, my dear friend, which you
have often promised, and I will promise Mrs.
Newman not to keep you any longer than you like
to stay. God bless you, my dearest friend, till we
meet. Let me hear from you soon. Eliza sends
her love to you, and Ianthe too. May you be
happy is the first wish of her who loves you
sincerely.

H. Shelley.

Write very soon and tell me if you have received
my last letter.

Letter XXII.

January 24th, [1815].

My dear Mrs. Nugent,

I am sorry to tell you my poor little boy has been very ill. He is better now, and the first spare time I devote to you. Why will you not come to England, my dear friend, and stay with me? I should be so happy to have you with me. I am truly miserable, my dear friend. I really see no termination to my sorrows. As to Mr. Shelley, I know nothing of him. He neither sends or comes to see me. I am still at my father's, which is very wretched. When I shall quit this house I know not. Everything goes against me. I am weary of my life. I am so restrained here that life is scarcely worth having. How I wish you were here. What will you do my dear Catherine?

Now those Newmans retire you will not like to go
to another house of business. The few years you
have to live may surely be passed more pleasantly.
Do now make up your mind at once to come and stay
with me. I will do everything to make you happy.
For myself happiness is fled. I live for others.
At nineteen I could descend a willing victim to
the tomb. How I wish those dear children had
never been born. They stay my fleeting spirit,
when it would be in another state. How many
there are who shudder at death. I have been so
near it that I feel no terrors. Mr. Shelley has
much to answer for. He has been the cause of
great misery to me and mine. I shall never live
with him again. 'Tis impossible. I have been so
deceived, so cruelly treated, that I can never forget
it. Oh no, with all the affections warm, a heart
devoted to him, and then to be so cruelly blighted.
Oh ! Catherine, you do not know what it is to be
left as I am, a prey to anguish, corroding sorrow,
with a mind too sensitive to other's pain. But I
will think no more. There is madness in thought.
Could I look into futurity for a short time how
gladly would I pierce the veil of mystery that
wraps my fate. Is it wrong, do you think, to put

an end to one's sorrows? I often think of it—all is so gloomy and desolate. Shall I find repose in another world? Oh grave, why do you not tell us what is beyond thee? Let me hear from you soon my dear friend. Your letters make me more happy. Tell me about Ireland. You know I love the green Isle and all its natives. Eliza joins in kind love to you. I remain your sincere but unhappy friend

H. SHELLEY.

LONDON : PRINTED FOR PRIVATE CIRCULATION ONLY: 1889.